CALLUM INNES **RESONANCE**

TATE ST IVES

This catalogue has been published
to accompany the exhibition

CALLUM INNES RESONANCE

22 January – 2 May 2005

ISBN 1 85437 592 X
A catalogue record for this publication
is available from the British Library

Edited by Susan Daniel-McElroy
and Kerry Rice
Design Groundwork, Skipton
Print + repro Jigsaw, Leeds

The exhibition has been funded by
Tate St Ives Members and Tate Members

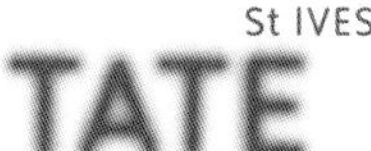

INTRODUCTION **CALLUM INNES** ON SUBTRACTION

Callum Innes' project to tease out the nature of the painting process in an ongoing series of canvases is a remarkable philosophical achievement of some fifteen years' endeavour. It might be fair to propose that any artist who becomes entranced with the very substance of their medium, can become bogged down in the cycle of analysis, dynamic eliminations and deconstruction and could end up in blind alleys of quotidian irony. Callum Innes belongs to a group of British artists who continue to contribute to the dialogue of painting at a time when it is not the main focus of contemporary practice.

To the interested eye, Innes' paintings express a number of paradoxes in their complexity. They engage our bodies in their relationship to our scale, but the surface of the *Resonance* series for example, is impossible to look at in one gaze. We have to move back and forth to look at their detailed and dappled surfaces. We can also see spatial depth contrasted with flat geometric structure in a number of series. Whilst works in all series appear to have a gravity or stillness, they simultaneously harness the energy of the vertical, intense colour or texture, causing the painted surface to expand dynamically in terms of the architectural drama inherent in the painting.

All of Innes' paintings propose construction and subtraction in the same register of looking. The *Exposed Painting* series in particular, presents a utopian purity which has subsequently been subverted by the imperfect behaviour of the painterly process. Innes has learnt much about the physical laws of paint applied to a canvas that is subtracted or eroded by dissolving, removing or staining with Turpentine. As objects these works are grounded in the visual language of art history. And the sense of time in these paintings is evident in the manner of their making; repeated and continuous meticulous strokes of the brush sweep the length of the canvas and we are reminded of the endurance and technical virtuosity of the artist's hand. These paintings have a remarkable emotive presence which is devoid of unnecessary elaboration, but at the same time Innes has avoided the trap of being precious, too perfect, too complete in his painterly subtraction.

We are indebted to Keith Hartley, Deputy Director of the Scottish National Gallery of Modern Art for his thoughtful essay on Innes' works and techniques and the context in which his work is seen. We are grateful to the artist's assistants for supporting the exhibition management in a swift and efficient manner. The artist's galleries, in Scotland, Ireland, America, Switzerland and England, have each made valuable contributions to this project; our thanks to Elsbeth Bisig, Darragh Hogan, Richard Ingleby, Sean Kelly and Jane Hamlyn in particular. As always, many Tate colleagues have been involved but our particular thanks are to Norman Pollard. Lastly, we are grateful to Callum Innes for his dedication to the creation of new works for this remarkable exhibition at Tate St Ives.

SUSAN DANIEL-McELROY

Director, Tate St Ives

THE ART OF CALLUM INNES **RESONANCE**

In principle abstraction offers the artist an almost infinite number of ways of painting a canvas. There would seem to be none of the limitations on form, colour or texture that representational art, by its very nature, imposes upon it. In practice, however, abstraction imposes its own, very specific, restrictions. Free, expressive or 'informal' abstraction can easily degenerate into arbitrary, self-indulgent mark-making, if it is not tied into some sort of overall structure, system or procedure which provide external reference points or validation. Such validating structures are, of course, central to all forms of geometrical abstraction; they are their *raison d'être*. Geometry is mathematically quantifiable. As such it belongs to that order of things that is not contingent on perceived reality, that is not subject to the general flux. Geometry and numbers are universals and in tying their art to them, abstract painters have sought to imbue their works with a sense of permanence and objectivity. This is not to say that all subjective emotion is extinguished. This would be impossible; nor would it be desirable. The aim is, rather, to channel feeling into a defined set of parameters and to endow these structures and the play between their individual parts with a dynamism that only emotional involvement can produce. Piet Mondrian's geometrical paintings are the prime examples of this type of abstraction. At first sight the austere configuration of their horizontal and vertical black lines, the relationships between plane and line, between plane and edge, between line and colour, between primary colours and white look as if they had been calculated mathematically and measured with a ruler. However, they were, in fact, arrived at intuitively. X-rays show that in many of Mondrian's paintings the lines were moved about until they reached their final placement, achieving maximum tension and a satisfying equilibrium. Mondrian felt his way to his compositions. Within the seemingly narrow and restricted confines that Mondrian had imposed on himself, he could concentrate his emotional involvement on creating the optimum relationship between the formal components at his disposal.

In similar fashion Callum Innes has established a small number of painterly strategies within whose restricting but at the same time liberating confines he has chosen to work for the past fifteen years or so. Exposed, monologue, formed, resonance, quotation, identified forms, isolated form: these are the names that Innes has given to these types of abstract painting. Each involves a very particular painting process, resulting in a characteristic structure, but common to them all is the centrality of the act of *removing* paint, as much as applying it in the first place. Innes began to make regular use of this technique at the beginning of the 1990s, after having been deeply impressed by the work of Lucio Fontana that he had seen in Amsterdam in 1988 while on a Scottish Arts Council Residency. Fontana's cutting of his canvases, either in the form of a slashed line or of a punctured hole, led Innes to the realisation that painting did not have to be a purely additive process, that lines, planes and colour did not have to be the result solely of a build-up of paint on the surface of a canvas, but that, by removing paint previously applied, he could create a multi-layered effect – not just in physical, but in temporal terms as well. Physically, the area from which paint has been removed, leaving a more or less visible residue, stands mid-way between the white ground and the areas of intact, opaque paint. This does not mean that the area from which paint has been removed will immediately be *read* as a mid-way point between ground and paint surface. In temporal terms, close reading of Innes's canvases will reveal the history of their making and show the sequence of events that produced the various layers of paint. The complex interweaving of perception and cognitive analysis, between immediacy and duration, between the physical and the imagined lie at the core of an appreciation of Innes's work. An examination of a few of the paintings in this present exhibition and of the categories to which they belong – exposed painting, monologue and resonance – will make this plain.

The 'exposed paintings' have become increasingly central to Innes's exploration of colour, surface, space and time in his work. In the early paintings of this category made at the beginning of the 1990s, Innes used only one colour, applied vertically and evenly to the whole of the canvas. He then used turpentine to remove nearly all of the paint from a predetermined section of the canvas – from top to bottom. A very faint residue of paint remained on one part of the canvas to show that there had actually been colour there in the first place. The two resultant, upright rectangles and the often dark colours (an almost black olive paint was a preferred choice) produced an austere geometry reminiscent at first glance of certain types of colour-field painting. However, on closer inspection the slightly ragged edge of the painted area and the unpredictable and random traces of paint on the other section of the canvas reveal or suggest (at least to the trained eye) that Innes is not simply concerned with geometrical proportion and colour perception, but with a slow and laborious process of revelation (exposure). Psychologically the physical act of removing paint is quite different from applying it. The latter involves creating something out of nothing, but also, and particularly in the case of abstract painting, it suggests covering up, concealment. The former suggests exposing something to view, the revelation of something hidden. In this respect there is something numinous about these early exposed paintings by Innes.

In the recent exposed paintings (such as those in this exhibition) Innes has become much more complex, both in his use of colour and in how he applies the paint. He no longer paints the whole canvas, but a horizontal band that divides the painting into two unequal halves. There are now usually two colours, applied one on top of the other. In nearly all cases the top layer completely hides the bottom layer, but in *Exposed Painting: Scheveningen Black / Cadmium Red Deep* (2004) the black still shows beneath the red like a dark bass chord in a piece of music. When the paint is removed by applying turpentine in regular repeated horizontal brushstrokes (the paint, by contrast, has been applied vertically) the top coat of paint usually disappears almost completely. Only traces of it can be found at the very top of the area from which paint has been removed, at the vertical edge of the canvas and at the lower vertical edge of the area of the canvas covered by the dripped residue of turpentine and paint. Sometimes the colour comes as quite a surprise, differing as it does so much from the top colour. Black emerges from beneath red, violet from black.

The other major difference from the earlier exposed paintings results from the use of a horizontal band of colour. When the paint has been removed (either on the right or the left), the dripping turpentine and paint stains the area below the horizontal band on that corresponding side. In this way a new dynamic is introduced, upsetting the geometrical symmetry of the composition but counterbalancing this through the contrast between strong opaque colour on the one side of the painting and a veil of washed-out colour on the other side. Just as Mondrian balances plane, line and colour in dynamic and taut compositions, so Innes sets up an equilibrium between the 'concealed' and exposed parts of his paintings.

Another consequence of using an horizontal band of colour is that Innes now causes us to relate ourselves, our bodies, to his compositions. The lower edge of the band corresponds roughly in height to the position of our hips, which is perhaps the principle point of articulation in our bodies. Below are our legs which root us to the ground; above are our torso, head and arms which stretch upwards and outwards into ambient space. Involuntarily our bodies relate to the way that Innes articulates the space and the ambiguities that he creates spatially. The stained area below the right rectangle in *Exposed Painting: Scheveningen Black / Cadmium Red Deep* or below the left rectangle in *Exposed Painting: Blue Violet / Charcoal Black* (2004) root our bodies downwards. On the other hand the push-pull of advancing and receding colours articulates our bodies forwards backwards and sideways into space. The red in *Scheveningen Black / Cadmium Red Deep* advances towards us, while the diluted black recedes – but not uniformly; at the top and bottom the black is much less intense and does not have the strong horizontal bands that the larger central section has. We are also aware visually of the black showing through the red rectangle. This all leads to strongly differentiated sensations of recession and a sense of keyed-up dynamism. If Innes's earlier exposed paintings have a numinous, static quality about them, his recent paintings are much more complex spatially and involve us more physically.

Innes's 'monologue paintings' are quite different in approach and effect. Geometry (at least in a conventional sense) does not figure in them at all. They simulate natural processes such as dripping or falling water. At first sight a painting like *Monologue Seven* (2003) looks as if Innes had simply thrown turpentine onto a painted canvas and allowed it to flow down the surface, eating away at the paint as it went. The unevenness of the 'bite' seems to vouch for its naturalness. The nearest equivalent in artistic terms to the 'monologues' are perhaps the poured paintings of Morris Louis or the *Schüttbilder* ('poured paintings') of the Viennese Actionist, Hermann Nitsch. The difference is that Louis's and Nitsch's paintings were the result of actual pourings; Innes's monologues are very carefully choreographed. Turpentine is applied to the painted surface of the canvas, but it is not allowed to drip down at random. It is coaxed and nudged by brushes in the direction desired by the artists. The other major difference is that Louis and Nitsch were adding paint (even if, in Louis's case, it was very thin and soaked into and stained the canvas, rather than sitting on top of it); Innes is taking it away. More than perhaps in any other of his subtractive works, it is in his monologues (particularly *Monologue Seven*) that Innes achieves a sense of breaking-through to another level, which may or not be spiritual, but is certainly mysterious. The meaning of the word monologue to designate this type of painting is not immediately apparent, but if does suggest a unitary composition, not conceived as a dialogue between two internal parts or a conversation between many. As such it is very fitting for a formal structure aping the unity of nature.

In his 'resonance paintings' Innes uses a different analogy (if only loosely): namely that of music. These works consist exclusively of white paint applied to a white ground. Turpentine is then used to remove thin vertical lines of paint creating a mottled effect of paint and (revealed) ground over the whole canvas. Because paint and ground are a similar shade of white, our ability to read the pattern of marks (or negative marks, since we are talking about removed rather than added paint) depends on the fall and angle of the light and on our moving in front of the canvas. As we move, the interaction of the glossy paint surfaces and adjacent matt ground, the former advancing towards us, the latter receding, resonates like notes of music. If we stand still and try to look at the whole painting, we are less conscious of the overall play of gloss and matt, perceiving it instead in isolated areas,

as our eyes scan the surface. This, in fact, encourages us to move about, in order to
appreciate the painting's overall structure. As with music, we are only able to take in the
whole of the work through time and memory. This is a key aspect of much of Innes work,
but especially true of the resonance paintings.

Looked at in its entirety, with all its various approaches and types of paintings, Innes's
work has the character of a grand project about it. Maybe not consciously and
deliberately, and certainly not in a calculating fashion, he has, in effect, analysed the state
of abstract painting in the late twentieth century, isolated a few of its salient characteristics
and processes and revivified them by introducing a new and quite revolutionary, painterly
procedure: subtraction, the removal of paint. Described in this way, it sounds like
postmodern, quotational painting which became popular in the 1980s – the Neo-Geo
painting of such artists as Peter Halley, come readily to mind – but Innes's work could not
be further removed from this highly self-conscious approach. There is a brittle artificiality
about most postmodern abstraction that is very different from what we perceive as a
naturalness, even organicism, in Innes's paintings. The geometry of his exposed paintings
is always tempered and grounded in the passage of time by the seemingly natural erasure
of paint. His monologue paintings look as if they had been produced by natural processes
like running water. Organicism and abstraction have a long history stretching back to
Art Nouveau and resurfacing in Surrealism (Miró and Masson) and culminating in its
locus classicus, the drip paintings of Jackson Pollock (who famously said 'I am Nature.').

Postmodern writers and theorists have stressed the artificiality and culturally conditioned nature of art; they have questioned the extent to which artists can express 'themselves' in their work. By presenting natural-looking processes and forms in his paintings (no matter how unnaturally they were produced), Innes is, in a sense, going against a trend in abstract art which emphasises the artificial. One thinks of David Reed for example. But he is very much part of a wider movement of artists who embrace repetition and rhythm in their paintings. Bernard Frieze and Juan Uslé come readily to mind. Innes is only too aware of the dangers of a false romanticism, of thinking that in his paintings he could recapture an innocent belief in nature. But he has not given up his belief in the restorative and uplifting powers of nature. He therefore treads a very fine line between artifice and illusion in his paintings. We, as viewers, can suspend disbelief for a while in enjoying the illusion of his 'natural' surfaces and structures, but then we question how these surfaces and structures were made, as we see tell-tale signs of their making. It is the constant backwards and forward between suspended disbelief – emotion – and analysis – inquiring intellect – that make Innes's paintings so rich.

KEITH HARTLEY

Senior Curator, Scottish National Gallery of Modern Art

Resonance Seventeen

2004
Oil on canvas
212.5 × 207.5 cm
Courtesy Sean Kelly Gallery, New York
© The Artist
Photo: Hyjdla Kosaniuk, 2004

Exposed Painting Lamp Black

2004
Oil on canvas
122.5 × 117.5 cm
Courtesy Frith Street Gallery, London
© The Artist
Photo: Hyjdla Kosaniuk, 2004

Exposed Painting Vine Black

2004
Oil on canvas
227.5 × 222.5 cm
Courtesy Ingleby Gallery, Edinburgh
© The Artist
Photo: Hyjdla Kosaniuk, 2004

Exposed Painting Blue Violet Charcoal Black

2004
Oil on canvas
227.5 × 222.5 cm
Courtesy Frith Street Gallery, London
© The Artist
Photo: Hyjdla Kosaniuk, 2004

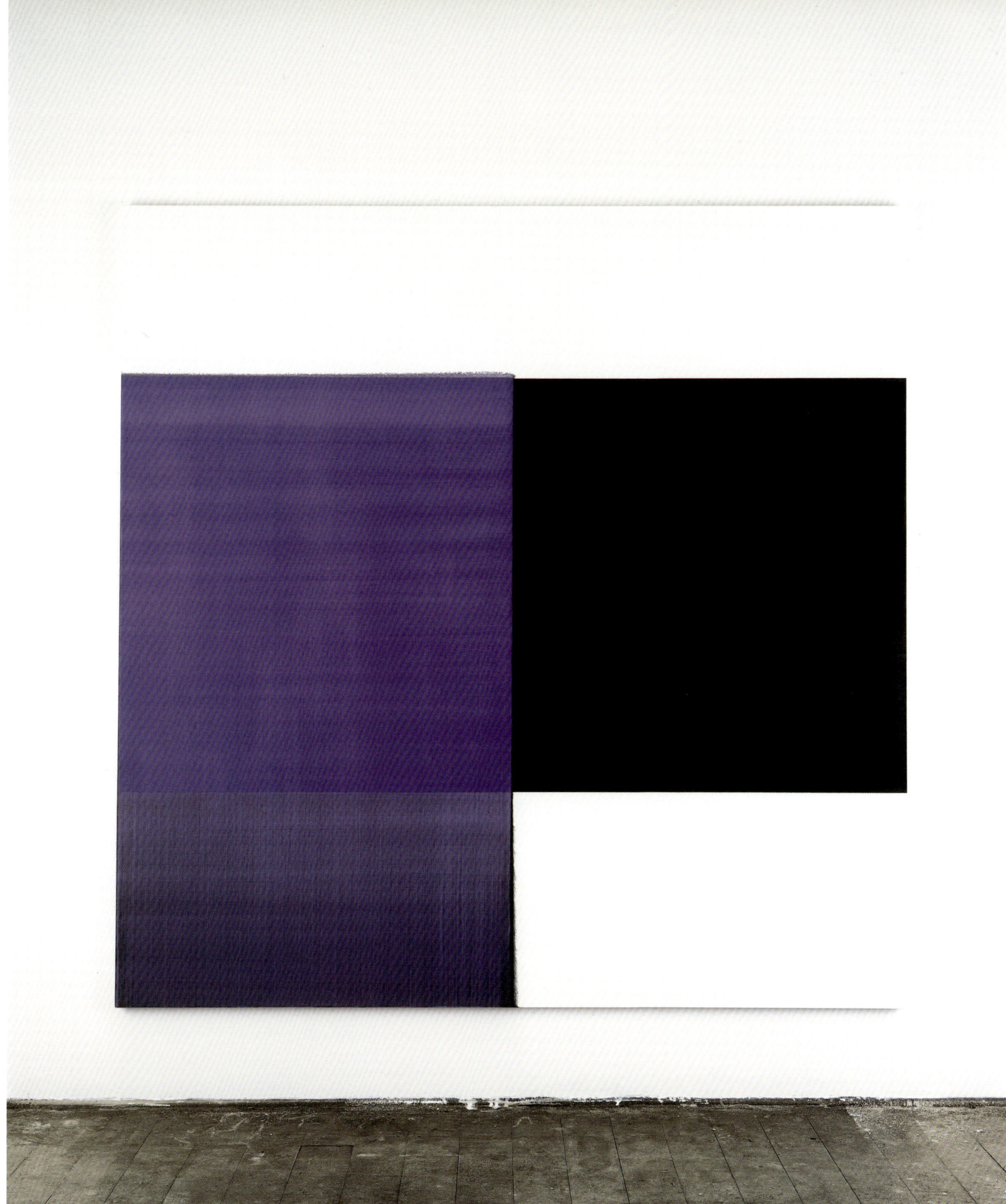

Exposed Painting Marrs Black

2004
Oil on canvas
227.5 × 222.5 cm
Courtesy Frith Street Gallery, London
© The Artist
Photo: Hyjdla Kosaniuk, 2004

Exposed Painting Dioxazine Violet Scheveningen Black

2004
Oil on canvas
227.5 × 222.5 cm
Courtesy Sean Kelly Gallery, New York
© The Artist
Photo: Hyjdla Kosaniuk, 2004

Exposed Painting Scheveningen Black Cadmium Red Deep

2004
Oil on canvas
174.5 × 164.5 cm
© The Artist
Photo: Hyjdla Kosaniuk, 2004

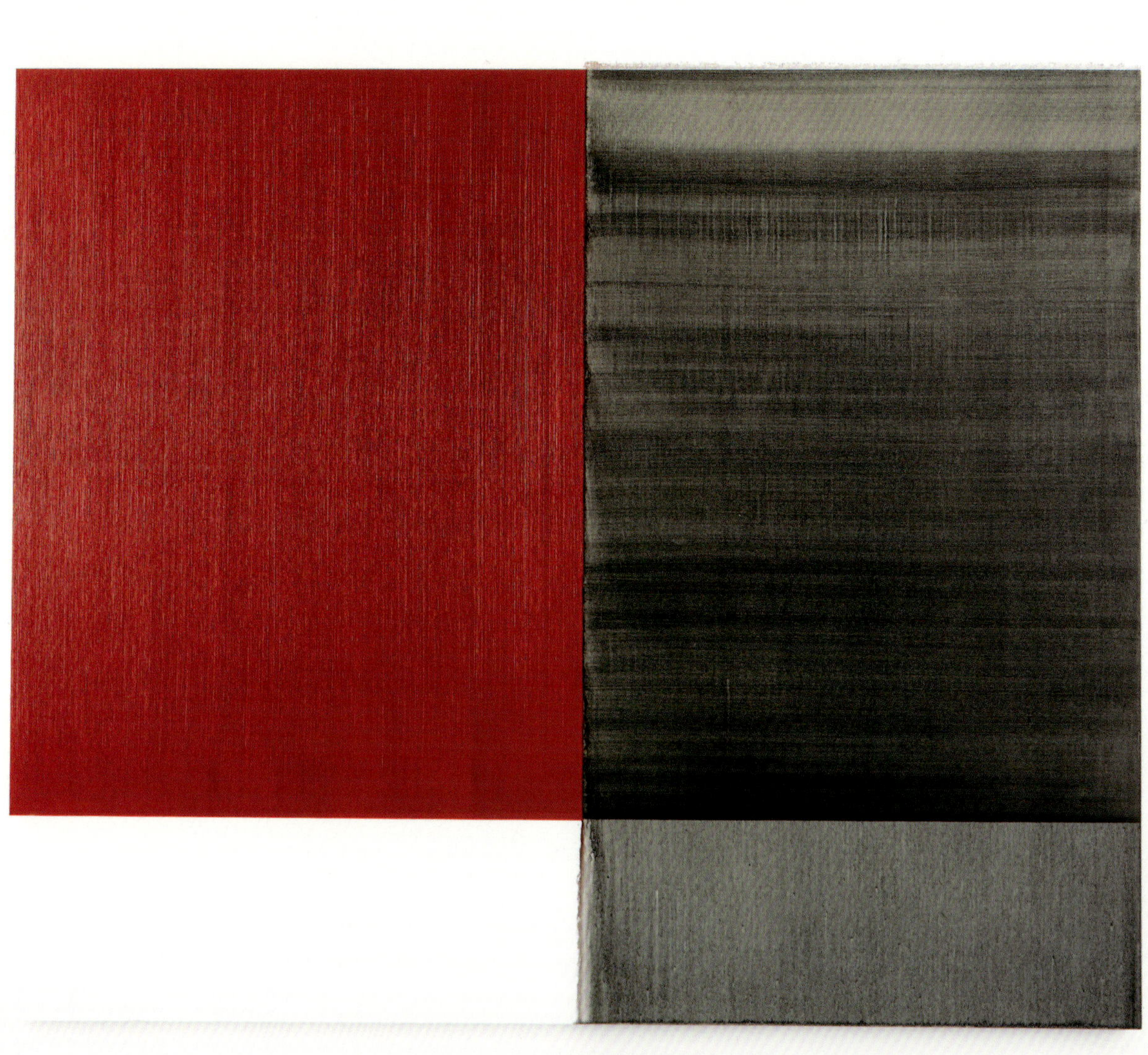

Exposed Painting Lamp Black

2004
Oil on linen
174.5 × 167.5 cm
Courtesy Frith Street Gallery, London
© The Artist
Photo: Hyjdla Kosaniuk, 2004

Agitated Vertical

2004
Oil on linen
174.5 × 162.5 cm
Courtesy Ingleby Gallery, Edinburgh
© The Artist
Photo: Hyjdla Kosaniuk, 2004

Exposed Painting Charcoal Black / Orange Oxide Painting

2003
Oil on linen
174.5 × 167.5 cm
Courtesy Frith Street Gallery, London
© The Artist
Photo: Hyjdla Kosaniuk, 2004

Exposed Painting Titanium White on White

2004
Oil on linen
174.5 × 162.5 cm
Courtesy Frith Street Gallery, London
© The Artist
Photo: Hyjdla Kosaniuk, 2004

Monologue Seven

2003
Oil on canvas
227.5 × 222.5 cm
Courtesy Kerlin Gallery, Dublin
© The Artist
Photo: Hyjdla Kosaniuk, 2004

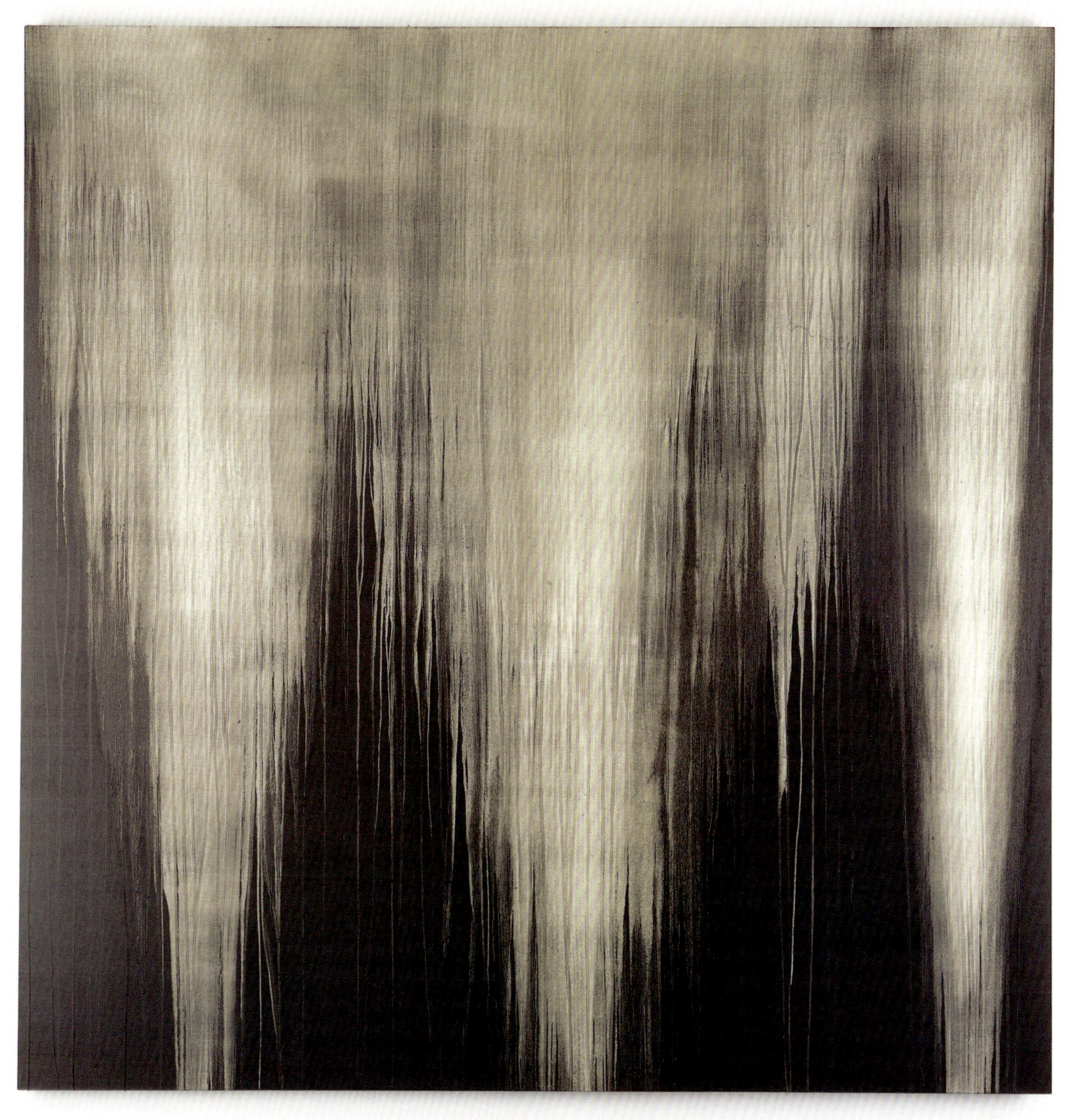

CALLUM INNES SELECTED BIOGRAPHY

1962 Born in Edinburgh

1980–84 Grays School of Art, Aberdeen.
Edinburgh College of Art, Post Graduate DIP
Shortlist Turner Prize

1998 Winner, Nat West Art Prize

2002 Winner, Jerwood Prize

2003 Awarded Honorary Doctorate, Aberdeen University

2004 Associate Member, Royal Scottish Academy

SELECTED SOLO EXHIBITIONS SINCE 1990

2004 Ingleby Gallery, Edinburgh, UK*
Galerie Tschudi Glarus, Switzerland
Kerlin Gallery, Dublin, Ireland

2003 *Callum Innes: Scheveningen Black*, Sean Kelly
Gallery, New York, USA

2002 Andrew Jensen Gallery, Auckland, New Zealand

2001 *Callum Innes: Exposed Paintings,* Ingleby Gallery,
Edinburgh, UK*
Frith Street Gallery, London, UK
2000 Sean Kelly Gallery, New York, USA
The Pier Arts Centre, Stromness, Orkney, UK
Kerlin Gallery, Dublin, Ireland
Jensen Gallery, Auckland, New Zealand

1999 Irish Museum of Modern Art, Dublin, Ireland*
Kunsthalle Bern, Switzerland*

1998 Sean Kelly Gallery, New York, USA
Ikon Gallery, Birmingham, UK*
Galerie Bob van Orsouw, Zürich, Switzerland
Frith Street Gallery, London, UK
Brownstone & Corréard, Paris, France

1997 Sean Kelly Gallery, New York, USA
Kunsthaus Zürich, Zürich, Switzerland
Galerie M. + R. Fricke, Düsseldorf and Berlin,
Germany

1996 Frith Street Gallery, London, UK
Patrick de Brock Gallery, Knokke, Belgium
Inverleith House, Royal Botanic Garden Edinburgh,
UK*
Galerie Slewe, Amsterdam, The Netherlands

1995 *The Turner Prize*, Tate Gallery, London, UK
Mackintosh Gallery, Glasgow School of Art,
Glasgow, UK
Galerie Gilbert Brownstone and Cie, Paris, France
Galerie M. + R. Fricke, Düsseldorf, Germany
Galerie Bob van Orsouw, Zürich, Switzerland
Angel Row Gallery, Nottingham, UK*
Galeria Paolo Gentili, Florence, Italy

1994 Frith Street Gallery, London (with Juan Uslé), UK

1993 Galerie Bob van Orsouw, Zürich, Switzerland
Jan Turner Gallery, Los Angeles, USA*
Galerie Patrick de Brock, Antwerp, Belgium

1992 I.C.A., London, UK*
Galerie nächst St. Stephan, Rosemarie
Schwartzwälder, Vienna, Austria
Scottish National Gallery of Modern Art,
Edinburgh, UK

1991 Frith Street Gallery, London, UK
Galerie Patrick de Brock, Antwerp, Belgium

1990 Frith Street Gallery, London, UK
Jan Turner Gallery, Los Angeles, USA

SELECTED GROUP EXHIBITIONS SINCE 1990

2004/05 WOW, Henry Art Gallery & Western Bridge,
Seattle, USA *

2004 *The Furniture of Poul Kjaerholm and Selected Art
Works*, Sean Kelly Gallery, New York, USA

*Singular Forms (Sometimes Repeated):
Art from 1951 to the Present,*

Solomon R. Guggenheim Museum, New York, USA*

The Edge of the Real, Whitechapel Art Gallery,
London, UK

C6 H 10 05, Andrew Jensen Gallery, Auckland,
New Zealand

Callum Innes and Bernard Frieze, Frith Street Gallery,
London, UK

White, Ingleby Gallery, Edinburgh, UK

*Reflections: Bernard Frieze, Prudencio Ibarazal and
Callum Innes,*

Galería Helga de Alvear, Madrid, Spain

Exodus, Kettles' Yard, Cambridge, UK *

2002 *Abstraction*, Ingleby Gallery, Edinburgh, UK*

Sphere (loans from nvisible Museum), Sir John
Soane's Museum, London, UK

Remarks on Color, Sean Kelly Gallery, New York,
USA

2001 *Fusion*, G Fine Art, Washington DC, USA

FRESH: Recent Acquisitions, Albright Knox Art
Gallery, Buffalo, USA

Six Degrees of Separation, Jensen Gallery, Auckland,
New Zealand *

Heads and Hands, Loans from the invisible Museum,
Washington Project for the Arts, Corcoran,
Washington DC, USA

Here and Now; Scottish Art 1990–2001, Dundee
Contemporary Arts, UK*

2000 *Kevin Appel, Jeremy Dickenson, Callum Innes,
Tom LaDuke, Linda Stark*, Angles Gallery,
Santa Monica, USA

On The Edge Of The Western World, invisible
Museum, London, travels to Museum of Modern
Art, San Francisco, USA

Blue: borrowed and new, The New Art Gallery,
Walsall, UK *

The Tao of Painting: Principles of Monochrome,
The McKinney Avenue

Contemporary, Dallas, USA

Expressions: Scottish Art 1976 – 1989, Dundee
Contemporary Arts, Dundee, Scotland

*A Century of Innocence – the history of the white
monochrome*, Rooseum Centre for Contemporary
Art, Malmö, Sweden*

1999 *Prime*, Dundee Contemporary Arts, Dundee,
Scotland*

New Work: Painting Today, Recent Acquisitions,
San Francisco Museum of Modern Art,
San Francisco, USA

1998 *1998 Nat West Art Prize – Prize Winner*, Lothbury
Gallery, London, UK

Abstract Painting, Once Removed, Contemporary
Arts Museum, Houston, travelled to Kemper
Museum of Contemporary Art, Kansas City, USA

Family, invisible Museum at Inverleith House in the
Royal Botanic Gardens, Edinburgh, UK

Slewe Galerie, Amsterdam, The Netherlands

Inner Eye – Contemporary Art, Marc and Livia
Straus Collection, Samuel

P. Harn Museum, Gainesville, USA

*Baltimore Collects, Four Corners Selections from
the Collection of Michael and Ilene Salcman.*
Stevenson, USA

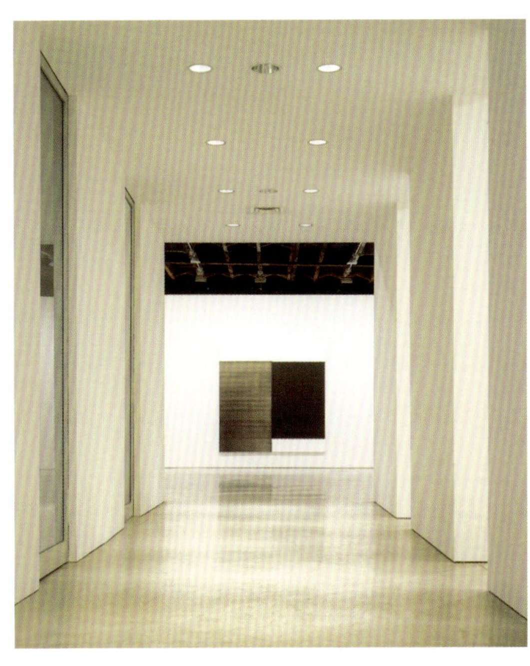

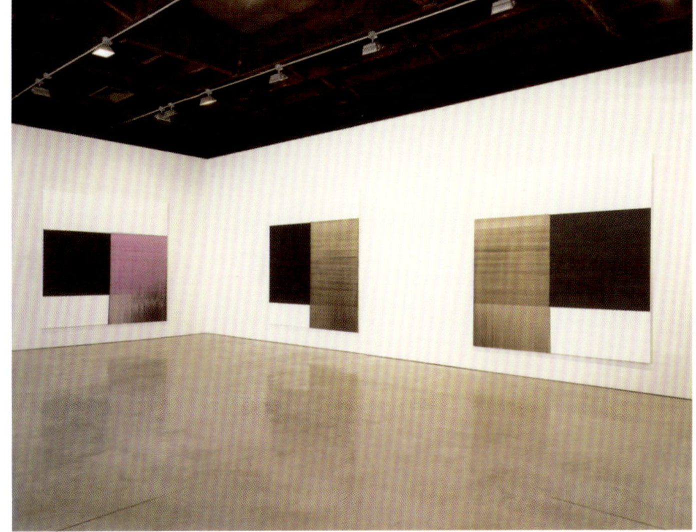

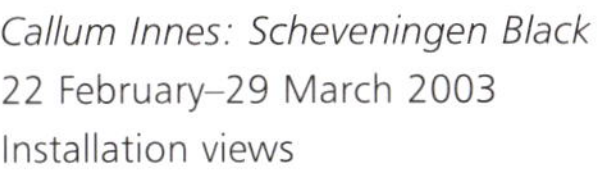

Callum Innes: Scheveningen Black
22 February–29 March 2003
Installation views
Courtesy Sean Kelly Gallery, New York
Photo: Steven Harris, New York

1998 *Family*, Inverleith House, Royal Botanical Garden, Edinburgh, UK

Infra-Slim Spaces, Birmingham Museum of Art, Birmingham, USA

Eroffnung des Jahresmuseum 1998, Kunsthaus Murzzuschlag, Germany

1997 *Best of the Season,* Aldrich Museum of Contemporary Art, Ridgefield, USA

Abstractions Provisoires, Musee d' Art Moderne de St. Etienne, St. Etienne, France*

Magnetic – Drawings in Dialogue, Sean Kelly Gallery, New York, USA

Seattle Collects Paintings, Seattle Art Museum, Seattle, USA

Absolut Vision: British painting in the '90's, The Fruitmarket Gallery, Edinburgh, UK*

John Moore's, Walker Art Gallery, Liverpool, UK*

1996 *Kleine Welten*, Galerie M. + R. Fricke, Düsseldorf, Germany

Leoncavallo, Milan, Italy

Absolut Vision: British painting in the 90's, Museum of Modern Art, Oxford, UK*

1995 *Jerwood Award for Painting*, Royal Scottish Academy, Edinburgh; Royal Academy, London, UK*

The Mutated Painting, Galerie Martina Detterer, Frankfurt, Germany

From Here, Karsten Schubert Gallery and Waddington Galleries, London, UK*

Architecture of the Mind, Galerie Barbara Farber, Amsterdam, The Netherlands*

New Abstraction, Kohn Turner Gallery, Los Angeles, USA

The Punter's Art Show, BBC Project, The Orchard Gallery, Derry, UK

1994 *New Voices*, Centre d'Art Santa Monica, Barcelona, travelled to Museo de Bellos Artes, Bilbao, and Madrid, Spain*

Delit d'initiés, Galerie Gilbert Brownstone and Cie, Paris, France

Lead and Follow; The Continuity of Abstraction, (Robert Loedear Collection) Atlantis Gallery, London, UK*

Paintmarks, Kettles Yard, Cambridge, travelled to City Art Gallery, Southampton and Mead Gallery, University of Warwick, Coventry, UK*

Collezione Agostino e Patrizia Re-Rebaudengo, Turin; La Galleria Civice di Modena, Modena, Italy*

Idea Europe, Palazzo Pubblico, Siena, Italy*

Seeing the Unseen, nvisible Museum, Peter Fleissig Collection, London, UK

The Curator's Egg, Anthony Reynolds Gallery, London, UK

1993 *Works on Paper*, Galerie nächst St. Stephan, Vienna, Austria

Prospect '93, Frankfurter Kunstverein und Schirnhalle, Frankfurt, Germany*

New Voices, Arts Council of Great Britain World Touring Exhibition, travelled to: Centre de Conferences Albert Borchette, Brussels, Belgium; Musée Nationale d'Histoire et d'Art, Luxembourg; Taksim Art Gallery, Istanbul, Turkey; State Fine Arts Gallery, Ankara; State Painting and Sculpture Museum, Izmir, Turkey

Moving into View; Recent British Painting, Arts Council of Great Britain touring exhibition.

John Moore's, Walker Art Gallery, Liverpool, UK*

Coalition, Center for Contemporary Arts, Glasgow, UK

Callum Innes / Perry Roberts: Works on Paper, Frith Street Gallery, London, UK

Wonderful Life, Lisson Gallery, London, UK

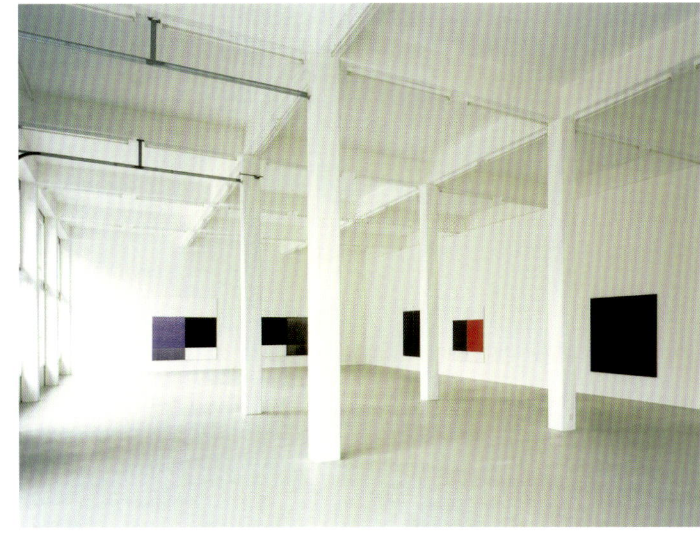

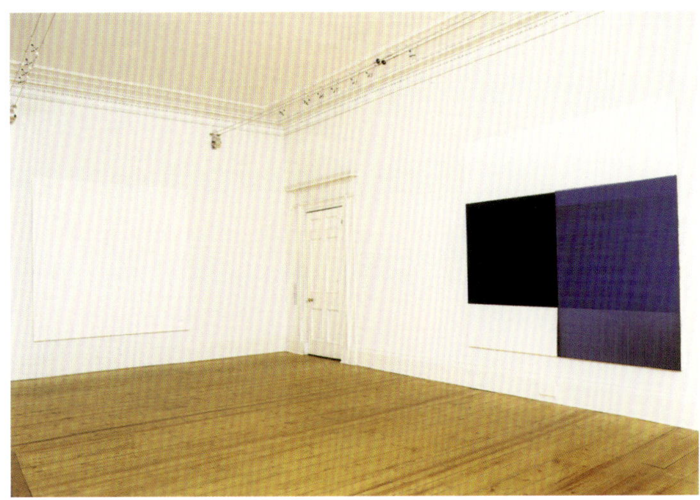

1992 *Abstrakte Malerei zwischen Analyse und Synthese*, Galerie nächst St. Stephan, Vienna, Austria*

Galleria L'Attico, Rome, Italy*

Johnen & Schöttle, Cologne, Germany

1991 *Painting Alone*, Pace Gallery, New York, USA*

Kunst Europa, Kunstverein Freiburg, Freiburg, Germany*

Artisti Invitati Al Premio Internazionale, (First Prize), Milan, Rome, London, USA Busche Galerie, Cologne, Germany

1990 *The British Art Show*, MacLellan Galleries, Glasgow, travelled to: Leeds City Art Gallery, Leeds, and the Hayward Gallery, London, UK*

SELECTED COLLECTIONS

Albright-Knox Art Gallery, Buffalo, USA

Arts Council of England

Birmingham City Museum & Art Gallery, Birmingham, UK

Birmingham Museum of Art, Birmingham, AL, USA

The Bohen Foundation, New York, USA

The British Arts Council, London, UK

City Art Centre, Edinburgh, UK

Contemporary Arts Museum, Houston, USA

Contemporary Arts Society, London, UK

Deutsche Bank, UK

Government Art Collection, UK

HypoVereinbank, Munich, Germany

Irish Museum of Modern Art, Dublin, Ireland

Kunsthaus Zurich, Switzerland

Kunsthalle Bern, Switzerland

Kunstmuseum Nuernberg, Germany

Modern Art Museum of Fort Worth, Fort Worth, USA

Musee des Beaux-Arts, Lausanne, Switzerland

National Galleries of Australia, Canberra, Australia

Neuberger & Berman Collection, New York, USA

Progressive Corporation, Cleveland, USA

Royal Bank of Scotland, UK

San Francisco Museum of Modern Art, USA

Scottish National Gallery Of Modern Art, Edinburgh, UK

Solomon R. Guggenheim Museum, New York, USA

Southampton City Art Gallery, UK

Tang Teaching Museum/Art Gallery, Skidmore College, Saratoga Springs, USA

Tate Gallery, London, UK

The Scottish Parliament, Edinburgh, UK

Towner Art Gallery and Museum, Eastbourne, UK

Walker Art Gallery, Liverpool, UK

* *denotes publication*

Atlantic Ocean from Tate St Ives
Photo: Bob Berry